Improving
Education Through
Action Research

The Practicing Administrator's Leadership Series
Jerry J. Herman and Janice L. Herman, Editors

ROADMAPS
TO SUCCESS

Other Titles in This Series Include:

(see back cover for additional titles)

Improving Education Through Action Research

A Guide for Administrators and Teachers

James E. McLean

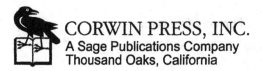
CORWIN PRESS, INC.
A Sage Publications Company
Thousand Oaks, California

For information address:

Corwin Press, Inc.
A Sage Publications Company
2455 Teller Road
Thousand Oaks, California 91320

SAGE Publications Ltd.
6 Bonhill Street
London EC2A 4PU
United Kingdom

SAGE Publications India Pvt. Ltd.
M-32 Market
Greater Kailash I
New Delhi 110 048 India

Printed in the United States of America

Library of Congress Cataloging-in-Publication Data

McLean, James E.
    Improving education through action research : a guide for administrators and teachers / James E. McLean.
        p.   cm. — (Roadmaps to success)
    Includes bibliographical references (p. 69-72)
    ISBN 0-8039-6186-3
    1. Action research in education—United States. 2. Action research in education—United States—Case studies. 3. School improvement programs—United States.   I. Title.   II. Series.
LB1028.24.M394   1994
370'.78—dc20   94-23860

This book is printed on acid-free paper.

99 10 9 8 7 6 5 4 3 2

Corwin Press Production Editor: S. Marlene Head

Contents

Foreword

Here is the handbook that will demystify the research process and allow teachers and administators to improve their teaching, schools, and school districts by using an action research approach.

Chapter 1 emphasizes the need for action research and illustrates the ease with which practitioners can take what they already know and, using an inexpensive computer program, scientifically investigate how to determine what is in the best interest of schools and students. It establishes the basic reasoning for implementing an action research approach to school improvement.

Chapter 2 discusses the kinds of strategy to use in school improvement efforts, how to measure the validity of the action research process, and ethical considerations that must be considered when conducting action research. Chapter 2 also presents detailed information on how to use an inexpensive computer software program called MYSTAT to analyze data. This chapter provides the detailed instruction necessary to analyze data using various types of simple statistical procedures.

Chapter 3 provides examples of a classroom action research study and a district-level action research study. In each case, detailed figures take the reader through the specific series of steps taken to explore the problem, collect and analyze the data, and draw conclusions from the data.

Chapter 4 provides a working model for conducting action research. In it, McLean discusses the far-reaching potential of action research as a means of improving schooling and schools.

In addition to a welcome annotated bibliography, numerous illustrations are provided. This book will be helpful for systematically exploring both the causes of problems in schools and the means for solving them.

JERRY J. HERMAN
JANICE L. HERMAN
Series Co-Editors

Preface

Classroom teachers and school administrators have had fad after fad thrown in their direction, each with the promise that this was the solution to their problems. Thousands and thousands of dollars go into the implementation of these fads, but reality never seems to achieve the promise. Action research is not a fad or a new curriculum; it is a reflective approach for making sound judgments about what we are doing. To be effective, there must be a long-term commitment to action research. Once we begin using an action research process, we stop searching for "the" answer and begin examining our current and future practices in a systematic way. The purpose of this book is to assist teachers and school administrators in adopting action research as a school improvement strategy and, by doing so, taking a more active role in determining what works best in our schools. As a "how-to" book, it does not attempt to address the role of action research in general theory development.

The book defines the origins and history of action research, presents an action research strategy and the methods for implementing that strategy, and provides detailed examples at the classroom and school system levels. The last chapter summarizes the action research model presented in the book.

The book offers help to teachers and administrators at two levels: First, for those who want to engage in action research, the book provides detailed directions to help one to become an independent action researcher; second, for those who are involved at a higher administrative level, it provides a model and helpful information about the benefits of action research and its proper interpretation.

I would be remiss if I did not thank several individuals and groups who made this book possible. First, I would like to thank Jerry J. Herman who suggested I write this book and gently prodded until I agreed. He also shared many ideas gained from his experience as a teacher, principal, and superintendent. Both Jerry and Janice L. Herman, series co-editors, made many useful suggestions for improving the book. I express my appreciation to Gracia Alkema, president, Ann McMartin, editor, and others at Corwin Press, Inc. for their support during the project and to SYSTAT, Inc. and Course Technologies, Inc. for providing software, books, and advice. Thanks to Anna Williams for her editorial suggestions and to Elizabeth McLean, who designed Figure 4.1. I also owe a debt to my own teachers, my students past and present, and many classroom teachers who shared their ideas about action research with me. Thanks to my family for their sacrifices and support during the completion of this writing project.

JAMES E. MCLEAN

About the Author

James E. McLean is actively engaged in working with teachers to define and implement action research projects. His formal education includes a Ph.D. in the foundations of education, a master's degree in statistics, and a B.S. in education from the University of Florida. He currently serves as Assistant Dean for Research and Service in the College of Education at the University of Alabama, where he promotes and coordinates research and service activities in the college. He was designated as a University Research Professor by the University of Alabama Board of Trustees in 1987. He also serves as co-editor of *Research in the Schools*. For the past 25 years, he has taught, researched, and administered programs that have included the direction, codirection, or administration of almost 100 research, assessment, and evaluation projects. Most of these projects have been conducted in public schools.

McLean has received the two highest teaching awards given by the university—the National Alumni Association Outstanding Commitment to Teaching Award (1991) and the Burlington Northern Foundation Faculty Achievement Award in Teaching (1989). His research has been recognized by Mensa Education and Research Foundation (1988-1989 Award for Excellence in Research), the Mid-South Educational Research Association (Outstanding Research

Paper Award in 1988, 1993 and 1994), and the American Educational Research Association (1981 Division H Award for the Best Report of an Evaluation Study). His students have won numerous awards for their research from the college and from professional associations.

Introduction

An examination of journals and textbooks in education reveals that most of the current theories and programs used in our schools are the products of college professors, not educational practitioners. Traditionally, teachers are given a prescribed curriculum and told how it should be implemented. Principals are promoted as instructional leaders but are seldom given the opportunity for much input into the selection of instructional materials or methods for which they must provide leadership. Teachers are seldom consulted about what has worked for them, and because very few classroom teachers or field administrators write the textbooks or produce the research articles on which the textbooks are based, their input into the curriculum and its implementation is severely limited.

Just as the Japanese car industry illustrated to the world that the involvement of their workers was related to the quality of the automobiles that were produced, teachers and school principals must be involved in the development of instructional processes if our children are to be well educated. This is not a new idea. John Dewey said that the best source of improved knowledge about teaching is the teachers. Action research is a method that taps this source of information and helps teachers and principals have a greater impact on learning. It also provides administrators with a process that promotes student learning and teacher and principal commitment.

Independent of the specific findings of action research studies, the process itself can have a positive effect on the entire education program. Action research requires teachers and principals to conceptualize problems, design studies, and closely observe outcomes. Sharing the results promotes even higher levels of thinking and conceptualization. Action research provides administrators with a process that encourages teachers to become more involved in curriculum design and committed to implementation of the findings. Further, action research can be the basis of one of the most effective professional development programs available. The action research process includes exploring previous research on the topic and closely observing student outcomes. Action research is a process by which teachers and administrators select the most effective teaching strategies and fine-tune them to fit their own situations. If used appropriately, action research leads to the maximization of student achievement.

Minimal new skills are required for teachers and administrators to begin using action research. Most of the necessary skills are common to every teacher education and administrator training pro-·gram. Action research can take advantage of data already obtained as part of the teaching-learning process. Analyses that may be required can be done using computers, simple microcomputer programs, and step-by-step instructions such as those provided in this book. Using these programs, teachers and administrators can take skills they already possess and apply them using a systematic strategy to make data-based educational decisions. Action researchers conceptualize the problem, gather and analyze the data, interpret the results, and use these results to improve practice.

Action research can have direct benefits for school and system administrators as well as the indirect effects previously noted. First, the empowerment of teachers and principals using action research brings the collective creativity and brainpower of the principal and the teachers to bear on a problem. Solutions are cooperatively arrived at and the involved teachers are committed to their implementation. The same processes used in the classrooms to solve classroom problems can be brought to bear on school and system problems. Several teachers and principals in the same school or in different schools can work cooperatively on a problem. Results can be compared and a common solution or solutions unique to each individual condition can be identified. The results of these studies can be used to solicit the support of parents, school boards, and the general public.

Implementation of a complete program of action research can lead to the improvement of education as has no other educational innovation of the past century. Action research is not a program or specific intervention, but a process for determining what works best. It equips every teacher and administrator with the necessary skills and with an attitude not to accept the status quo, but to ask, "Is there a better way?" A teacher or administrator trained in action research feels empowered because he or she is no longer merely the consumer of research or the products of other people; the action researcher can determine for him- or herself if the new widget is right or wrong for his or her situation. Action research puts the teacher and school administrator on an equal footing with textbook authors, curriculum developers, and educational theorists.

Aside from the empowering aspects of action research, there is an even more important reason teachers and principals should become familiar with it. That is, no matter how conclusive research findings are about a particular innovation, it may not be applicable in every context. Thus action research should be used with any new program to determine if it is valid and if it is better than past practice for that particular school's or school district's application. This same concept holds for current practice. Is it good because we have been doing it a long time, or is it good because we have tangible evidence of its worth?

Action Research Defined

Action research is the process of systematically evaluating the consequences of educational decisions and adjusting practice to maximize effectiveness. This involves teachers and school administrators' delineating their teaching and leadership strategies, identifying their potential outcomes, and observing whether these outcomes do, indeed, occur. Essentially, action research is examining one's own practice. Action research is a process that promotes the positive impact that teachers and administrators have on student achievement. Action research takes maximum advantage of the assumption that the best sources of effective educational practice are those most directly involved with teaching—teachers and principals.

The Origins of Action Research

The concept of *action research* is historically credited to Kurt Lewin in the post-World War II 1940s. It emerged from the field of social psychology promoted primarily by Lewin to study "minority problems." It was extended to industrial training by a former student of Lewin's who became his colleague, Ronald Lippitt. In the early 1950s, Lewin's and Lippitt's ideas were adopted and applied to the educational arena by Stephen Corey, Dean of Teachers College, Columbia University. He encouraged teachers, principals, and supervisors to use action research to improve their own practices. During this period, the development of *sensitivity training* was attributed directly to action research methods.

The popularity of action research led to its use by social scientists as well as by practitioners. Its popularity brought action research under the scrutiny of the scientific establishment that rejected it as a less rigorous, small-scale version of experimental research, rather than as an alternative for practitioners. In the face of this criticism, its popularity declined in the late 1950s and early 1960s just as quickly as it had risen.

Action research began to reemerge in the 1970s based on work by Lawrence Stenhouse and John Elliott. They expanded Corey's concept of action research by emphasizing its aim as adding to the understanding of the solution and the development of a theory of teaching as well as solving practical problems. Many of the results of action research studies are reported as case studies. Stenhouse and others argue that it is possible to generalize the results of action research case studies by accumulating and synthesizing the findings.

Action research has the potential to improve practice and provide teachers and principals with a deeper understanding of the teaching process. At the very least, it provides a process for weighing educational alternatives and making decisions.

Why Should School Administrators Support Action Research?

Implementation of an action research program at a school provides numerous benefits for the principal, teachers, and students. Although action research is not a quick fix for all school problems, it represents a process that can lead to the selection of the best option for each specific situation. It provides teachers, individually and collectively, with greater flexibility, greater knowledge, and greater self-satisfaction. The result is a school with a more knowledgeable and motivated professional staff. Because action research is a process, not a program, it can be applied to any new problem that might emerge, and it can be used to evaluate and select the most effective educational alternatives for the school. The teachers and principal become equal partners with curriculum developers and educational theorists in deciding what works best in their situation. So although action research is not a quick fix, it can promote a model school where student achievement is moving toward its potential under the guidance of a highly motivated and self-assured professional staff. From strictly a principal's standpoint, implementing an action research program can focus the brainpower of the entire instructional staff on maximizing learning. It can make a winning team who will make decisions that will benefit the school's and school district's students.

Action Research Methods

One concern that teachers and principals have about becoming involved in action research is that they do not possess the proper skills. Fortunately, most skills needed to perform action research are known already. The skills are the same ones needed to assess student learning, assign grades, and make administrative decisions. Additionally, one must possess a desire to improve the practice of education to be an effective action researcher.

Action research is the process of evaluating the effectiveness of materials and processes used to achieve student learning. Even if a teacher or school adopts a nationally recognized and validated program, the program may not work in a particular school or classroom, or it may need to be modified to gain maximum advantage. Teachers and principals are the best ones to make these judgments. The judgments should be based on more than "it feels good" criteria. That is, we should design procedures into our teaching to evaluate its effectiveness just as we include methods to evaluate how well our students learn. Each individual situation is different, and what works well in one situation (or even in most situations) may not work well in all situations. The people closest to the students are in the best position to make these judgments based on personal observation and decision making.

An Action Research Strategy

A strategy for implementing action research can be viewed as having three phases: *conceptualization, implementation,* and *interpretation.* The conceptualization and interpretation phases of action research require only skills that are part of every good teacher's and every good administrator's repertoires. The implementation phase builds on those skills. The primary new skill is the ability to compare the performance levels of groups of students. However, these skills are closely related to skills already used by teachers and principals for analyzing and reporting performance. In addition, the new skills needed for these tasks are greatly reduced by the availability of technology. This chapter provides detailed instructions about how to complete this task effectively.

It is imperative to conceptualize the research before it is begun. Conceptualization requires careful consideration of what constitutes the particular teaching-learning or administrative process under study (inputs), what results it is expected to promote (outcomes), and how the inputs might promote the outcomes. The research is conceptualized by considering the inputs of the education or administrative process and how these inputs will manifest themselves in the outcomes. Action research is the process of determining if this happened. In many cases, just the process of carefully considering the inputs and outcomes brings about a clearer understanding and leads to ideas of how the process can be improved.

The implementation phase of the strategy has three components: *measurement of the outcomes, identifying a standard of comparison,* and *comparing current performance with the standard.* This is the most technical phase of action research, but it does not have to be unduly complicated. Recent developments in technology can greatly reduce the difficulty of this phase. Specific guidance for completing the required tasks in this phase is provided in the next section.

The third and final phase of action research is interpretation. It is during this phase that judgments are made about the effectiveness of the practice under study. This phase brings together the findings of the research from the second phase with the conceptualization from the first phase. Not only can judgments be made about whether the present practice produces better results than the comparison but other questions about practical significance and cost-effectiveness of this practice are also appropriate.

The basic strategy of action research requires that the conceptualization, implementation, and interpretation phases be completed in that order. The implementation phase requires that additional detail be provided before it can be done. It is during this phase that the data needed for conducting action research are actually gathered and analyzed. The next section provides details regarding these activities.

Implementing the Action Research Strategy

Implementation of the action research strategy has three steps. Although the information needed for two of these steps is readily available to most teachers and administrators, it is seldom examined from the perspective of improving instruction or administrative decisions.

The first step is the measurement of the outcomes identified in the conceptualization phase. Fortunately, this is generally done anyway by most teachers and administrators, but it is usually done in terms of individual students and not in terms of a classroom or school. Because grades are often based, at least in part, on test scores or other student assignments, measurement of these outcomes already takes place. It is often possible to identify measures of the outcomes that would have been available even if they were not used for action research. Such data may be available from sources such as school, system, and state assessment programs. At the upper grade levels, scores from college admissions tests and vocational tests may be used to measure desired outcomes of instruction. Even the proportion of students electing to take such tests or those electing to enroll in postsecondary education may provide information relating to the outcomes of instruction. Noncognitive measures such as attendance, tardiness, and election of advanced courses also may serve as excellent outcome measures.

The second step in the action research process is identifying a standard of comparison. If the outcomes were based on instructional objectives, this may be as simple as describing the performance criteria in terms of the measurement in the first step. However, in most cases, we will want to use a standard based on the performance of students on the same or similar measures. Such a comparison group may be similar students during the same time period, the same students at a time prior to the current study, or other students at a time prior to the present study (for example, the previous year's class). If the measure is a standardized test, the test norming group may serve as a standard of performance.

The third step is comparing current performance with the standard. The comparison of performance can be as simple as counting the number of students who equaled or exceeded the standard. The nature of this type of research does not require the use of sophisticated inferential statistics. Comparisons can be made using simple descriptive statistics such as graphs and numerical descriptive measures. These computations can be done quite efficiently using inexpensive microcomputer software that does not require the decision maker to possess statistical training and requires only a rudimentary knowledge of the computer.

Comparing Performance

Comparing the performance of a current class or group with a previous class or other comparison group requires the most technical skills of those needed to conduct action research, but it does not have to be overly complicated or labor intensive. However, if the skills involved have not been covered directly by teacher education or principal training programs, additional information is provided in its own section. The labor and technical expertise needed to make these comparisons is reduced considerably by modern technology, particularly microcomputers and recent analysis software.

One of the best and most versatile examples of analysis software is the SYSTAT family of products. SYSTAT has developed statistical analysis software that not only takes the drudgery out of the analysis but also makes it quite simple to do. SYSTAT has three levels of programs. Their full-featured statistical analysis software,

SYSTAT, can be used to do the simplest analyses to the most sophisticated. This package costs several hundred dollars, but it provides all the statistical power needed by most professional statisticians. SYSTAT is also available in a student version called Student SYSTAT that accompanies a book published by Course Technology, Inc. This book not only serves as a manual for the software but also provides excellent explanations of many statistical procedures. The complete package (book and software) costs approximately $50. SYSTAT, Inc. also has developed MYSTAT, an entry-level analysis package. MYSTAT is also available with a book from Course Technology, Inc. The book and software cost approximately $20. Both Student SYSTAT and MYSTAT are subsets of the full SYSTAT program. If the need to step up to the next version arises, there is no need to learn a new package; the higher level versions operate in similar fashions. All three versions of the SYSTAT software are available for DOS operating systems, Windows, and Macintosh computers. Additional information, including addresses and phone numbers of the companies, is in the Annotated Bibliography and References (see Berk, 1994; Hale, 1992; and SPSS Inc., 1992).

This book illustrates methods for comparing the performance of a treatment group with a comparison group and other appropriate procedures using an example and MYSTAT for Windows. Although the illustrations in this book use the Windows version of MYSTAT, it should be noted that the software commands would be about the same if one were using Student SYSTAT for Windows or SYSTAT for Windows. The commands are also very similar for the Macintosh version and the DOS version. The DOS version does require that the commands be entered through the keyboard rather than selected with a mouse pointing device. The commands are similar enough that there should be no problem in transferring among the versions.

The purpose of the example used in this chapter is to illustrate the analyses that may be appropriate in action research. The chapter that follows provides more complete examples of applying the entire action research strategy to a classroom and a school system. However, it seems appropriate to introduce the procedures with a less complex example.

The Textbook Example

Suppose that Ms. A. Researcher introduced a new textbook into the class. This textbook included many new hands-on student exercises when compared with the textbook previously used. The new text placed a major emphasis on higher order learning, and the exercises required that the students solve problems. At the end of the semester, the teacher, Ms. Researcher, gave this class the same exam given to the previous class that used the old text. She also had aptitude scores on each student available from the students' records and determined if the next class selected by both groups of students was an advanced class or a regular class.

We will refer to the group that used the new text as the treatment group and the group that used the old text as the comparison group. To keep the example simple, let us assume that there are 15 students in the treatment group and 14 students in the comparison group. Table 2.1 presents the achievement scores that the students made on the test, the aptitude scores that were obtained from the records, and whether each student selected an advanced class to follow.

We will look at two primary approaches for describing the set of scores and for comparing these groups. The first is a graphical approach, and the second is a numerical approach. The graphical approaches for describing a set of data and comparing groups to be covered are histograms (commonly referred to as bar charts), stem-and-leaf graphs, and box plots. All three graphs present similar information, and the choice is primarily a personal one. The method for depicting the relationship between scores is a scatterplot. This type of graph depicts how one score changes in relation to another score. The numerical methods for describing a set of data and for comparing groups are methods to describe the central tendency and variability of a set of scores. A numerical comparison technique will also be illustrated using a contingency table. A contingency table shows all possible outcomes when both variables are categorical in nature (e.g., group membership). A correlation coefficient will be presented to index the relationship between two sets of scores.

TABLE 2.1 Achievement Test and Aptitude Scores by Group

Treatment			Comparison		
Achieve-ment	Aptitude	Advanced[a]	Achieve-ment	Aptitude	Advanced[a]
83	99	Yes	77	100	No
81	90	No	76	91	No
84	119	Yes	79	121	No
80	80	Yes	79	108	No
82	99	No	77	110	No
81	90	Yes	78	102	Yes
82	98	Yes	76	91	No
82	108	Yes	78	109	No
80	89	No	75	84	No
81	96	Yes	76	98	No
79	72	No	77	101	No
83	110	Yes	80	129	Yes
85	128	Yes	75	82	No
83	118	Yes	74	73	No
82	107	Yes			

a. Yes indicates the student enrolled in an advanced class, and No indicates the student did not.

How to Enter Data

MYSTAT for Windows (and MYSTAT for DOS and MYSTAT for Macintosh computers) provides excellent analysis software, particularly for those who do not want to learn the hand calculation formulas. It eliminates the need to be able to compute the statistics, but it does not eliminate the need to understand what statistics to use in each situation. Computing the graphs and statistics with MYSTAT is quite straightforward and sets us free to learn when to use each procedure. MYSTAT for Windows will be used to illustrate the data analyses in this book. However, the Macintosh version is very similar and uses the same procedures, and the DOS version uses the same commands, but they must be entered through the keyboard.

The textbook evaluation example is used to illustrate how to use MYSTAT for analyses useful in action research. Detailed instructions are provided, but this book is not intended to replace the book that accompanies MYSTAT (Hale, 1992; Steagall and Hale for the Windows version, 1994). The instructions for completing each task are summarized in figures. To assist in understanding the instructions, all MYSTAT commands are listed in **bold** type. The Windows and Macintosh version of MYSTAT are controlled through the use of a mouse pointing device. The mouse is used to point a cursor on the screen at small pictures (icons) that represent the various functions of the program. When the cursor is pointed at the correct icon, a push of the button on the mouse (click) activates the procedure.

MYSTAT is started by pointing the cursor at the MYSTAT icon and double clicking the button on the mouse. The procedure is summarized in Figure 2.1. The MYSTAT Main window is now open with the MYSTAT Worksheet superimposed in the foreground (see Figure 2.2). The MYSTAT Main window and the MYSTAT Worksheet window in the foreground are two of the three main windows available in MYSTAT. The third is the Graph window used to display graphs when they are constructed. To move to a window other than the one that is showing, select **Window** from any of the window main menus that appear across the top of each window, followed by the choice of window (**Worksheet, Graph,** or **Main**). Notepad is also a choice, but it will not be used in this book. An alternate method of changing windows is to point the cursor to any portion of a window that is showing on the screen and click once. The window where the cursor was pointed when it was clicked will immediately move to the foreground.

To use MYSTAT or any analysis software, the data must be entered into the computer. MYSTAT makes it easy to enter data by providing the previously mentioned MYSTAT Worksheet (see Figure 2.2) that is very similar to a computer spreadsheet. Anyone familiar with a computer spreadsheet program will be right at home with the MYSTAT Worksheet. The names of the variables are entered across the top of the Worksheet. Variables will include "grouping variables" or variables that define which group a student belongs to and "numerical variables" that represent the values obtained on a test or observed numerical outcomes. In our

---

STARTING MYSTAT FOR WINDOWS

1. Double click on the **MYSTAT** icon in its Windows applications group.

2. MYSTAT is now ready for use.

Note: To select a window other than the one that is currently in the foreground, place the mouse pointer on any portion of a window that is showing and click once. That window will come to the foreground. An alternative method is to select **Window** on the MYSTAT Main menu followed by the desired window (**Worksheet, Graph,** or **Main**).

Figure 2.1. Starting MYSTAT for Windows

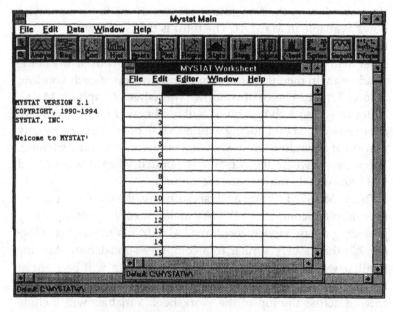

Figure 2.2. MYSTAT Worksheet Window in Foreground and Main Window in Background

example, we have four variables—the group students are in (treatment or comparison), the achievement score, the aptitude score, and a notation of whether each student signed up for an advanced version of the next class (yes or no). The first and the last variables are grouping variables and the middle two are numerical variables. MYSTAT allows us to name variables using up to eight letters and/or numbers, but the name must begin with a letter. Variable values may be numerical (a number) or text. Text variable names are used to name grouping variables and must end with a dollar sign ($). For our example, we will call our variables GROUP$, ACHIEVE, APTITUDE, and ADVENRL$. Note that GROUP$ and ADVENRL$ (our grouping variables) are text variable names and ACHIEVE and APTITUDE are numerical variable names.

Let us assume that we have an empty Worksheet (as in Figure 2.2) and are going to enter the data from our example. Figure 2.3 summarizes the steps that are needed. Place the mouse pointer in the first column just above Row 1 and click once. This will activate the cursor in that box. The names of the variables will be entered in this first row. Enter GROUP$ and tab to the next column. Now, enter ACHIEVE, tab to the next column, enter APTITUDE, tab to the next column, and enter ADVENRL$. We are now ready to enter our data. Place the mouse pointer in the box just below GROUP$ and click once. The data for each student are entered into a separate row with the values of a specific variable entered under the name of that variable or observation. Note that each column represents a specific variable and each row represents a specific student. The first student is in the treatment group so we enter TREATMNT in that box. (The word, TREATMENT, has been shortened to TREATMNT because MYSTAT will print only eight letters for the name of the level of a variable. Likewise, COMPARISON was shortened to COMPARSN.) Tab to the next box and enter that student's achievement score. In this case, it is 83. Tab once more and enter the aptitude score (99). Finally, tab and enter YES to indicate this student did enroll in the advanced section of the next course. Another tab will bring us back to Row 2 under GROUP$. Now we are ready to enter the data for the second student. This is repeated until the data for all 29 students are entered. At this time, it would be a good

ENTERING AND SAVING DATA

1. Select **Windows** followed by Worksheet from the
    MYSTAT Main menu bar
    or
    select **File** followed by **New** from the MYSTAT Main
    menu bar.

2. Enter one variable name at the top of each column.
    Variable names can be no longer than eight characters
    (letters and numbers) but must begin with a letter.
    Variable names of grouping variables must end in a
    dollar sign ($).

3. The MYSTAT Worksheet is now available to input
    data. Enter data in the appropriate cells. Each value
    must be entered under its appropriate variable name
    and to the right of its observation number. That is,
    each column represents a specific variable and each row
    represents an individual observation or score.

4. Data can be saved by selecting **File** followed by **Save
    as** from the MYSTAT Worksheet menu bar. In the
    dialog box that appears, enter the file name in the File
    Name box and select the storage location (disk drive
    and director). Select **Save** and the data will be saved in
    the specified location.

Figure 2.3. Entering and Saving Data in MYSTAT

idea to check the data to make sure they were entered correctly.
Corrections can be made by using the mouse pointer to select the
cell where a correction is to be made, clicking once, and entering
the correct value. Once the data are entered, the MYSTAT Worksheet appears as shown in Figure 2.4.

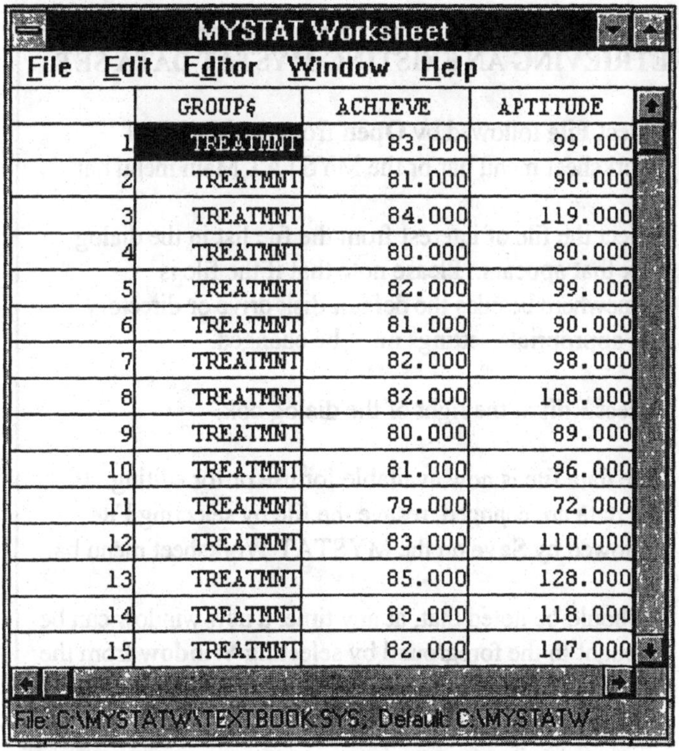

		GROUP$	ACHIEVE	APTITUDE	
	1	TREATMNT	83.000	99.000	
	2	TREATMNT	81.000	90.000	
	3	TREATMNT	84.000	119.000	
	4	TREATMNT	80.000	80.000	
	5	TREATMNT	82.000	99.000	
	6	TREATMNT	81.000	90.000	
	7	TREATMNT	82.000	98.000	
	8	TREATMNT	82.000	108.000	
	9	TREATMNT	80.000	89.000	
	10	TREATMNT	81.000	96.000	
	11	TREATMNT	79.000	72.000	
	12	TREATMNT	83.000	110.000	
	13	TREATMNT	85.000	128.000	
	14	TREATMNT	83.000	118.000	
	15	TREATMNT	82.000	107.000	

MYSTAT Worksheet

File   Edit   Editor   Window   Help

File: C:\MYSTATW\TEXTBOOK.SYS; Default C:\MYSTATW\

Figure 2.4. MYSTAT Worksheet Window With Textbook Example Data Entered

At this time, it is a good practice to save the data. The data are saved by selecting **File** in the MYSTAT Worksheet followed by **Save as**. When the dialog box is opened, select a name for the file and enter it in the File Name box. If the file is to be saved anywhere other than the default disk drive and directory, make that selection and then click on **Save**. Saved data may be retrieved at any time for further analysis or modification by following the procedures in Figure 2.5. Select **File** followed by **Open** from the MYSTAT Worksheet menu bar or the Main menu bar. Once the file dialog box is open, select the desired file and click on **Edit**. The MYSTAT Worksheet will appear with the data included.

RETRIEVING AN EXISTING MYSTAT DATA SET

1. Select **File** followed by **Open** from the MYSTAT
    Worksheet menu bar or the MYSTAT Main menu bar.

2. Select the file of interest from the file list in the dialog
    box that appears. Please note that if the file is
    somewhere besides the default disk drive or directory,
    the appropriate settings must be changed.

3. Select **Edit** at the right of the dialog box.

4. The data file is now available for use or for editing. If
    the data are changed, resave the file by selecting **File**
    followed by **Save** on the MYSTAT Worksheet menu bar.

5. It should be noted that, at any time, a new window can be
    brought to the foreground by selecting **Window** from the
    MYSTAT Main menu bar and clicking on the desired
    window (**Worksheet, Graph,** or **Main**).

Figure 2.5. Retrieving an Existing MYSTAT Data Set

Graphical Analysis Methods

Now that MYSTAT is activated and the data are entered, let us
turn our attention to analyzing the data. We will demonstrate
analyses that will be appropriate for most situations. First, we will
cover graphical techniques. Graphical techniques are used to describe sets of data graphically. Graphical techniques can be used to
describe a single set of data, compare two sets of data, or depict a
relationship between two variables in a set of data.

The first graphical procedure demonstrated is the histogram,
commonly known as a bar graph. The histogram is familiar to most
educators and is one of the most easily interpreted graphs for describing a single set of data. The basic histogram includes a hori-

zontal axis that represents the scores and a vertical axis that shows the number of occurrences (numbers or counts) or the proportion of occurrences (relative number of times a score occurs). Because a histogram is best for showing one set of data at a time, first let us learn how to select one of our two groups (treatment or comparison) to graph. To accomplish this, click on **Editor** that appears on the menu bar of the MYSTAT Worksheet (see Figures 2.4 and 2.6). Then, click on **Select cases** and a dialog box will appear. In the dialog box, click on the variable that includes the values to be selected (in this case **GROUP$**). Select **Add** to have the variable name inserted into the Select box. From the keyboard, insert an equals sign (=) followed by the word 'TREATMNT' enclosed in single quotes. Recall that TREATMNT is the label we used to designate our treatment group. Therefore, TREATMNT was inserted under the variable GROUP$ for each student who was in the treatment group. To activate the selection process, click on **OK**. A bullet (•) will appear to the left of each case that has been selected. Any analyses that are done to the data set will include only those selected cases. By selecting **Window** followed by **Main** on the MYSTAT Main menu bar, we return to the main window. We are now ready to construct a histogram for the treatment group.

A histogram is constructed by clicking on the histogram icon in the MYSTAT Main window (see Figure 2.7 for a summary of the instructions). It is also marked **Hist**. This will open a dialog box with the names of all numerical variables in the upper left-hand corner. Our variable of interest is achievement so click on **ACHIEVE** to highlight that variable and click on **Add→** to insert ACHIEVE into the Add box. Click on **OK** and the histogram is constructed and appears in a Graph window (see Figure 2.8). We can put a label on the graph by selecting the large **A** from the tools palette and clicking again where we would like the label to begin. Suppose we wish to put the label Treatment Group at the top of the histogram. Select the **A** from the tools palette and then place the cursor at the upper left-hand side of the histogram and click again. Now input from the keyboard Treatment Group (see Figure 2.9). To compare these results with those from the comparison group, the process must be repeated with the data from the comparison group. This is done exactly as it was for the treatment group data except that

---

SELECTING CASES

1. From the MYSTAT Worksheet, select **Editor** followed by **Select cases** to open the Select Cases dialog box.

2. Click on the variable of interest followed by the **Add** under the File box to insert it into the Select box.

3. From the keyboard, insert an equals sign (=) followed by the value of the variable of interest. If the variable is a grouping variable (ends in $), the value must be enclosed in single quote marks (' ').

4. To select the cases, click on **OK**. The cases that have been selected will be denoted by a bullet (●). Any analyses that follow will be done only with the selected cases.

5. Before other values of this variable can be selected or all of the data can be used again, the data-marked cases must be unselected. To unselect, click on **Editor** followed by **Select off** in the MYSTAT Worksheet.

Figure 2.6. Selecting Cases Using the MYSTAT Worksheet

the comparison group data are selected. To do this, the treatment group data must be unselected. Cases are unselected by clicking on **Editor** in the MYSTAT Worksheet and then clicking on **Select off**. Figure 2.10 shows the histograms for the treatment and comparison groups next to each other.

Another useful graph for depicting one set of scores or comparing two groups is the stem-and-leaf graph. It is constructed almost identically to the histogram except that it is begun by selecting the stem-and-leaf graph icon (denoted **Stem**) in the MYSTAT Main window (see Figure 2.11). Again, this would be done for the data

---

CONSTRUCTING HISTOGRAMS

1. Make sure that the appropriate data set is active and the group to be included in the histogram is selected.

2. Select the histogram icon (**Hist**) from the MYSTAT Main icon menu bar.

3. Click on the name of the variable to be graphed.

4. Select **Add→** to move the selected variable into the Add box.

5. Select **OK** to construct the graph.

6. Once the graph is constructed, it is possible to enhance the graph by selecting from the tools palette that appears at the top of the MYSTAT Graph box. This is done by selecting from among the icons. The first icon is the letter "A" that provides the ability to type labels on the graph. This is done by clicking on the "A" and then clicking on the graph at the location where the label is to start. The label is then input from the keyboard.

Figure 2.7. Constructing Histograms Using MYSTAT

in each group separately. Suppose we have already selected the treatment group cases. Select the **Stem** icon from the MYSTAT Main window to get the stem-and-leaf graph dialog box. Just as with the histogram, highlight **ACHIEVE** and click on **Add→** to place ACHIEVE in the Add box. Then, Select **OK** to construct the stem-and-leaf graph. Figure 2.12 depicts the resulting stem-and-leaf graph that appears in the MYSTAT Graph window and the other information that appears in the MYSTAT Main window. It is so named because the vertical axis labels or "stems" are comprised

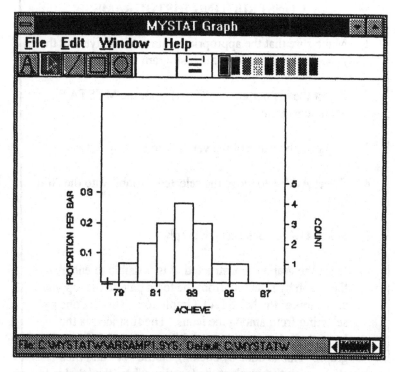

Figure 2.8. Histogram in MYSTAT Graph Window

of the tens digit of the numbers (in some cases it may be units, tens, hundreds, etc. depending on the data), and the bars are composed of the units digit of the numbers (called leaves). These are labeled in Figure 2.13.

Some people favor the stem-and-leaf graph over the histogram because it includes more information. For example, the original values of the variables can be determined by putting the stems and leaves back together. Close inspection will show that one of the stem values is marked with an M and one on each side is marked with an H. The M indicates the median or middle value (the value with 50% of the scores above and 50% of the scores below it) is

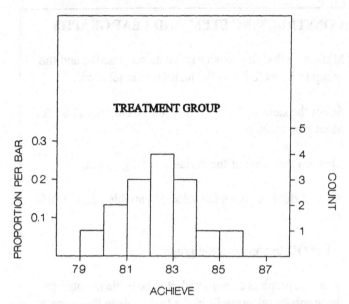

Figure 2.9. Histogram With Label TREATMENT GROUP Inserted

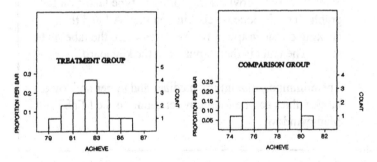

Figure 2.10. Histograms for Treatment and Comparison Groups

contained in that group of values. The H stands for hinge value. The hinge values identify the points that separate the lower 25% of the scores from the upper 75% and the upper 25% from the lower 75%. Thus the H and M values divide the set of scores into four parts each with 25% of the scores. The stems marked with the Hs

CONSTRUCTING STEM-AND-LEAF GRAPHS

1. Make sure that the appropriate data set is active and the group to be included in the histogram is selected.

2. Select the stem-and-leaf icon (**Stem**) from the MYSTAT Main icon menu bar.

3. Click on the name of the variable to be graphed.

4. Select **Add→** to move the selected variable into the Add box.

5. Select **OK** to construct the graph.

6. Once the graph is constructed, it is possible to enhance the graph by selecting from the tools palette that appears at the top of the MYSTAT Graph box. This is done by selecting from among the icons. The first icon is the letter "A" that provides the ability to type labels on the graph. This is done by clicking on the "A" and then clicking on the graph at the location where the label is to start. The label is then input from the keyboard.

7. The minimum, maximum, median, and upper and lower hinge values can be found by returning to the MYSTAT Main window.

Figure 2.11. Constructing Stem-and-Leaf Graphs Using MYSTAT

include the upper and lower hinge values. When the stem-and-leaf graphs were being drawn in the Graph window, other information was being entered into the MYSTAT Main window. By selecting **Window** followed by **Main** in the MYSTAT Graph window, the actual values of the lower and upper hinges and the median are displayed (as shown in Figure 2.12). Also displayed are the mini-

```
7   9
8   00
8H  111
8M  2222
8H  333
8   4
8   5
```

```
STEM AND LEAF PLOT OF VARIABLE:   ACHIEVE,    N = 15
```

```
MINIMUM IS:            79.
LOWER HINGE IS :             81.
MEDIAN IS:                   82.
UPPER HINGE IS:                    83.
MAXIMUM IS:        85.
```

Figure 2.12. Stem-and-Leaf Graph for the Treatment Group

STEM LEAVES

```
7   9
8   00
8H  111      ←LOWER HINGE
8M  2222
8H  333      ←UPPER HINGE
8   4
8   5
```

Figure 2.13. Stem-and-Leaf Graph With Stems and Leaves Labeled

mum and maximum values and the number of observations. Because the stem-and-leaf graph provides the same information as the histogram (the shape of the distribution of scores) plus the ability to recover the original scores and divides the distribution into quarters, it is generally preferred over the histogram. Figure 2.14 depicts the treatment and comparison group achievement scores using stem-and-leaf graphs. Note that both the hinges and the median in the treatment group are larger than their counterparts in the comparison group.

TREATMENT	COMPARISON
7 9	7 4
8 00	7 55
8H 111	7H 666
8M 2222	7M 777
8H 333	7H 88
8 4	7 99
8 5	8 0

Figure 2.14. Stem-and-Leaf Graphs for Both the Treatment and Comparison Groups

Another useful graph, particularly for comparing more than one set of data, is the box-and-whiskers plot or box plot for short. The box plot is so-called because, when the lines formed by the upper and lower H values are connected by two other lines, the resulting graph resembles a box. This box is enhanced by adding another line for the median and extending tails (whiskers) to represent the spread of the data. More specifically, whiskers extend up to one and one half times the distance between the upper and lower hinges (referred to as the Hspread). Thus, if the data do not vary much from the center, the whiskers do not extend the full one and one half Hspreads from the box. The box plot is constructed in a similar manner to a histogram or stem-and-leaf graph using MYSTAT except that it is begun by selecting the box icon (**Box**) from the MYSTAT Main icon bar (see Figure 2.15). Click on the variable to be graphed (**ACHIEVE** in this case) followed by **Add→** to place it in the Add box. If multiple graphs are to be constructed, for example, one for each group, click on the group variable (**GROUP$** in this case) followed by **GROUP→**. Figure 2.16 represents a box slot of the treatment group achievement scores from our example. The various components noted previously have been labeled.

The data from our example do not vary beyond the whiskers in the box plot. In some cases, data do not behave so well. An advantage of the box plot is its ability to depict data points that vary beyond one and one half Hspread units from the box. If a data point is outside the one and one half Hspreads but still within three Hspreads, it is denoted with an asterisk (*). If a data point is more

---

CONSTRUCTING BOX PLOTS

1. Make sure that the appropriate data set is active or that a single group is not selected if multiple groups are to be plotted.

2. Select the box icon (**Box**) from the MYSTAT Main icon menu bar.

3. Click on the name of the variable to be graphed.

4. Select **Add→** to move the selected variable into the Add box.

5. If multiple groups are to be plotted simultaneously, select the grouping variable and click on **GROUP→** to insert it into the group box.

6. Select **OK** to construct the graph.

7. Once the graph is constructed, it is possible to enhance the graph by selecting from the tools palette that appears at the top of the MYSTAT Graph box. This is done by selecting from among the icons. The first icon is the letter "A" that provides the ability to type labels on the graph. This is done by clicking on the "A" and then clicking on the graph at the location where the label is to start. The label is then input from the keyboard.

Figure 2.15. Constructing Box Plots Using MYSTAT

than three Hspread units beyond the box, it is denoted with a zero (0). To illustrate these extreme values, let us change the first two achievement scores in our example to 100 (from 83) and 90 (from 81). Figure 2.17 depicts the box plot with the modified data.

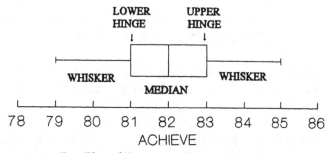

Figure 2.16. Box Plot of Treatment Group With the Components Labeled

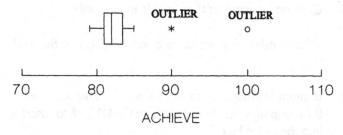

Figure 2.17. Box Plot of Treatment Group With Modified Data

Note that the 90 is denoted by an * as it is between one and one half Hspreads from the box, and the 100 is denoted by a 0 as it is beyond three Hspreads from the box. Data points that are beyond the whiskers are referred to as outliers. The fact that a data point is an outlier is not bad per se, but it does suggest that the data point may be in error and should be checked. For example, the data point could have been entered or recorded incorrectly (e.g., an 80 entered as an 8 or an 800). It could have come from a student who did not finish the exam because of illness or any one of many other reasons. The point is that outliers should be checked, particularly those that are denoted by a 0. If the data point is determined to be in error, it should be corrected or deleted. Data points that are not found to be in error should be retained in the analysis.

Another advantage of the box plot is that more than one group can be plotted on the same graph beside one another. This is extremely helpful for comparing two groups. Unlike a histogram or stem-and-leaf graph, box plots can be graphed simultaneously us-

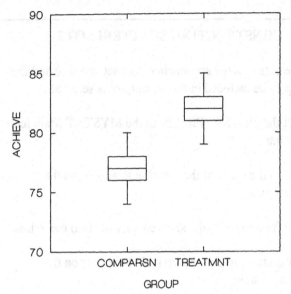

Figure 2.18. Simultaneous Box Plots of the Treatment and Comparison Groups

ing MYSTAT. This is done by highlighting and moving the grouping variable into the Group box after selecting the graphing variable. Figure 2.18 illustrates the results of plotting the achievement scores from our example for both the treatment and comparison groups simultaneously.

Because the two box plots are on the same scale, the two groups can be compared directly. First, it can be seen that there are no outliers in the data. Note how the box portions of the two graphs do not overlap. The upper whiskers portion of the comparison group plot overlaps with the lower portion of the treatment group plot between about 79 and 81. Because these portions represent less than 25% of the data in both groups, it can be deduced that most of the students in the treatment group outperformed most of the students in the comparison group.

The three graphical techniques that have been presented to this point are to describe either a single set of data or to compare the data from two groups. In some action research, the purpose is to describe the relationship between two sets of data for the same

CONSTRUCTING SCATTERPLOTS

1. Make sure that the appropriate data set is active and the group to be included in the scatterplot is selected.

2. Select the plot icon (**Plot**) from the MYSTAT Main icon menu bar.

3. Click on the name of the variable to appear on the vertical axis.

4. Select **Y→** to move the selected variable into the Y box.

5. Click on the name of the variable to appear on the horizontal axis.

6. Select **X→** to move the selected variable into the X box.

7. Select **OK** to construct the graph.

8. Once the graph is constructed, it is possible to enhance the graph by selecting from the tools palette that appears at the top of the MYSTAT Graph box. This is done by selecting from among the icons. The first icon is the letter "A" that provides the ability to type labels on the graph. This is done by clicking on the "A" and then clicking on the graph at the location where the label is to start. The label is then input from the keyboard.

Figure 2.19. Constructing Scatterplots Using MYSTAT

group. In our example, we might want to look at the relationship between the achievement scores and the aptitude scores in the treatment group. An appropriate method for doing this is a scatterplot. A scatterplot is a two-dimensional graph that provides a picture of the relationship between two variables. Before constructing the scatterplot, let us select the TREATMNT group only. This was

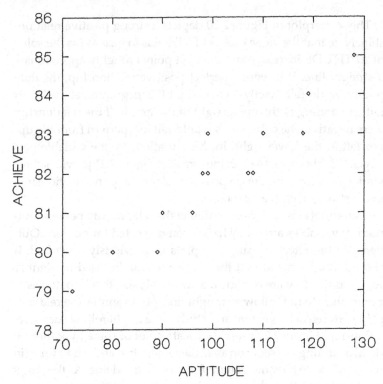

Figure 2.20. Scatterplot of ACHIEVE and APTITUDE for the Treatment Group

summarized in Figure 2.6 and is done by clicking on **Editor** in the MYSTAT Worksheet menu followed by **Select cases.** Highlighting **GROUP$,** clicking on **Add,** and inputting =TREATMNT from the keyboard completes the process. To construct a scatterplot, select the plot icon (**Plot**) on the MYSTAT Main icon bar (see Figure 2.19). This will open the Plot dialog box. On the two-dimensional graph, the Y-axis is the vertical axis and the X-axis is the horizontal axis. We will highlight **ACHIEVE** that we want to be on the vertical axis (it really does not matter if ACHIEVE or APTITUDE were chosen) and then click on **Y→** to insert the variable in the Y box. Then high-light **APTITUDE** (or **ACHIEVE** if APTITUDE was selected for the Y box) and click on **X→** to insert APTITUDE in the X box. Clicking on **OK** will draw the scatterplot. The resulting scatterplot is shown in Figure 2.20.

The scatterplot in Figure 2.20 depicts a strong positive relationship. Note that the value of ACHIEVE tends to increase as the value of APTITUDE increases and the data points roughly approximate a straight line. If it were a perfect positive relationship, the data points would fall exactly on a straight line beginning at the lower left and ending at the upper right of the graph. If the relationship were negative, the data points would fall in a pattern from the upper left to the lower right. In this situation, as one variable gets larger, the other variable becomes smaller. Figure 2.21 provides three scatterplots for a moderate positive relationship, no relationship, and a strong negative relationship.

Scatterplots are best used to depict the relationship between numerical variables after they have been inspected for outliers. Outliers can be detected using box plots as previously described. It should also be noted that the scatterplot can be used to identify relationships that are nonlinear as well as linear, that is, patterns of points that do not follow a straight line. For example, the relationship between achievement and study time might follow such a relationship. Figure 2.22 presents a scatterplot of some hypothetical data, including the score on an achievement test and study time (in minutes). Note how the pattern follows a curved line. As the study time increases, the achievement increases at a higher rate.

Using graphs is an effective method of analyzing data in action research. Another approach is to use numerical methods. The next section describes how similar analyses can be done using numerical descriptive methods.

Numerical Analysis Methods

Although graphs provide us with quick insights into the data, sometimes it is more convenient to use numerical descriptive measures. Most often, graphs and numerical measures are used together to support conclusions. We will present several types of numerical measures that describe the central tendency and variability in a set of data and the relationship between two variables.

The central tendency of a set of data was described previously using a stem-and-leaf graph and box plot that included the median, or the point that has 50% of the scores below it and above it.

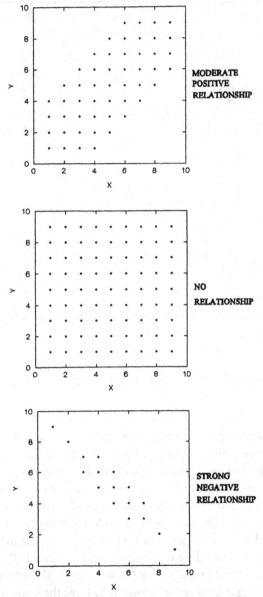

Figure 2.21. Scatterplots of a Moderate Positive Relationship, No Relationship, and a Strong Negative Relationship

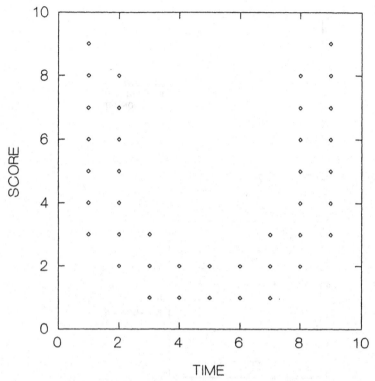

Figure 2.22. Scatterplot of Curvilinear Relationship

A median is unaffected by changes in the extreme scores. This can be an advantage or a disadvantage. When a set of data has outliers that can be verified as legitimate scores, estimating central tendency with the median may reduce bias. In most cases, it is best to use a measure of central tendency that uses the value of each score in the computation. Such a measure of central tendency is the mean. The mean is the arithmetic average, and it is computed by taking the sum of the scores and dividing it by the number of scores in the set.

A measure of central tendency by itself is not sufficient to describe a set of scores. Many sets of scores may have the same mean (or median) yet be very different. The difference may be due to the variability of the scores. Recall that Hspread, the difference between the upper and lower hinge values, was used in constructing a stem-and-leaf graph and box plot. Hspread is a measure of variability, but like the median, it is unaffected by extreme scores, and its computation is not affected by the value of all observations. A numerical measure of variability that uses the value of each score in its computation is the standard deviation. Although the hand computation of the standard deviation is tedious, it can be easily computed using MYSTAT and adds considerable meaning to the understanding of a set of data.

In most sets of data (particularly those that are mound shaped), about 68% of the scores fall between one standard deviation below the mean and one standard deviation above the mean. About 95% of the scores fall within two standard deviations of the mean, and almost all of the scores (99.7%) fall within three standard deviations. In some irregularly shaped sets of data, these exact percentages will not hold, but no less than 75% of the scores will fall within two standard deviations of the mean under any conditions, and at least 89% will fall within three standard deviations. Thus knowing the mean and the standard deviation of a set of scores can paint a mental picture of the entire set. For example, the mean and standard deviation of the major scales on the Kaufman Assessment Battery for Children (K-ABC), a popular intelligence test, are 100 and 15, respectively. Knowing just these two values tells us that about 68% of all children will have IQs between 85 and 115, 95% will have IQs between 70 and 130, and almost the whole population (99.7%) will have IQs between 55 and 145. The mean and standard deviation are usually used together to describe a set of data. For unusually shaped sets of data, the median and Hspread may also be used.

We have already seen how MYSTAT can compute the median and Hspread. They are depicted in both the stem-and-leaf graph and the box plot. Computing the mean and standard deviation is just as easy. If we want the numerical measures for just one group (say, the treatment group), we would first select that group as previously shown. Computing the mean and standard deviation is begun by selecting the statistics icon (**Stats**) on the icon menu bar of the MYSTAT Main window and opening the Descriptive Statistics dialog box (see Figure 2.23).

COMPUTING DESCRIPTIVE STATISTICS

1. Make sure that the appropriate data set is active and the group to be included in the analysis is selected.

2. Select the Statistics icon (**Stats**) from the MYSTAT Main icon menu bar.

3. Click on the name of the variable (or variables) to be analyzed.

4. Select **Add→** to move the selected variable into the Add box.

5. Direct the mouse pointer to the boxes beside each statistic that is desired and click. Clicking on one that already has an ✕ will unselect that statistic.

6. Select **OK** to compute the statistics.

7. The results will appear in the MYSTAT Main window.

Figure 2.23. Computing Descriptive Statistics Using the MYSTAT Stats Procedure

From the Descriptive Statistics dialog box, select the variables that are to be analyzed from the File box and click on **Add→** to add them to the Add box. Specific statistics to be computed can be selected by clicking the box beside the ones on the list that are desired. When this is done, an ✕ will appear in each box selected as the selection is made. Note that, as a default, ✕s already appear beside Maximum, Mean, Minimum, and SD. SD stands for standard deviation. It might be a good idea also to select Median and Range (the difference between the Maximum and Minimum values). To compute the statistics, click on **OK**. The statistics are computed and appear in the MYSTAT Main window. The number of cases analyzed is automatically displayed. Figure 2.24 displays the

```
TOTAL OBSERVATIONS:        15


                     ACHIEVE      APTITUDE

N OF CASES                15            15
MINIMUM               79.000        72.000
MAXIMUM               85.000       128.000
RANGE                  6.000        56.000
MEAN                  81.867       100.200
STANDARD DEV           1.598        15.138
MEDIAN                82.000        99.000
```

Figure 2.24. Descriptive Statistics for the Treatment Group

Descriptive Statistics output for the treatment group. Normally, this would be repeated for the comparison group.

A more efficient method to compute the statistics for both groups at the same time is to select the t-test icon (**t-test**) rather than the statistics icon (**Stats**). This procedure will produce some results that are not needed, but it reduces the labor as the procedure is run only one time rather than for each group separately. As noted, the first step is to select the t-test icon (**t-test**) from the MYSTAT Main menu (see Figure 2.25). In the dialog box that appears, select the variable (or variables) that is (are) to be analyzed from the File box (in this case, **ACHIEVE**) and select **Add→** to move it to the Add box. Next, select the grouping variable (in this case, **GROUP\$**) and select **GROUP→** to insert it into the Group box. Selecting **OK** will compute the statistics. The results are displayed in Figure 2.26. Using the t-test procedure produces sample sizes, means, standard deviations, and some other statistics that are beyond the scope of this book. The statistics it does produce are the major ones of interest, and it computes them with much less effort than executing the **Stats** procedure twice in conjunction with each selection process.

Numerical descriptive statistics provide information similar to that provided by the histograms, stem-and-leaf graphs, and box plots. Note that the mean of the treatment group is 81.9, whereas the mean of the comparison group is 76.9. This represents a difference of five points in favor of the treatment group. The standard

---

COMPUTING DESCRIPTIVE STATISTICS
USING MYSTAT T-TEST PROCEDURE

1. Make sure that the appropriate data set is active.

2. Select the t-test icon (**t-test**) from the MYSTAT Main icon menu bar to open the t-tests dialog box.

3. Click on the name of the variable to be analyzed.

4. Select **Add➡** to move the selected variable into the Add box.

5. Select the grouping variable and click on **GROUP➡** to insert it into the group box.

6. Select **OK** to compute the statistics.

7. The results will appear in the MYSTAT Main window.

Figure 2.25. Computing Descriptive Statistics Using the MYSTAT t-Test Procedure

```
INDEPENDENT SAMPLES T-TEST ON ACHIEVE GROUPED BY GROUP$

  GROUP        N      MEAN        SD
TREATMNT      15    81.867      1.598
COMPARSN      14    76.929      1.730

SEPARATE VARIANCES T = 7.968 DF = 26.4 PROB =  0.000
   POOLED VARIANCES T = 7.991 DF = 27   PROB =  0.000
```

Figure 2.26. Descriptive Statistics Using the t-Test Procedure

deviations are similar to one another (1.60 and 1.73 for the treatment and comparison groups, respectively). The means and standard deviations considered together suggest there is some overlap of the sets of data (they do not differ by more than six standard

---

EFFECT SIZE FORMULA

$$= \frac{(MEAN\ OF\ TREATMENT\ GROUP) - (MEAN\ OF\ COMPARISON\ GROUP)}{STANDARD\ DEVIATION\ OF\ COMPARISON\ GROUP}$$

$$= \frac{81.9 - 76.9}{1.73}$$

$$= 2.89$$

Figure 2.27. Hand Computation of Effect Size for Textbook Evaluation Example

deviations—three for each group), but they do differ by about three standard deviations. A more systematic method of interpreting the meaningfulness of differences is to compute its effect size. The effect size is the difference between the treatment and comparison group means divided by the standard deviation of the control group. It can be expressed as a formula and computed for our example as shown in Figure 2.27. Thus the effect size for our example is 2.89. The interpretation of effect size is somewhat subjective, but some general guidelines can be provided. Any effect size that exceeds 1.0 can be considered large and suggests that the difference is meaningful. An effect size of less than .50 is small and suggests that the difference is probably not meaningful. An effect size between .50 and 1.0 is moderate, and one must use caution when interpreting its meaningfulness. In our example, 2.89 is a large effect size and the difference should be considered meaningful. In other words, achievement of students who used the new textbook was meaningfully better than was the achievement of those students who used the old textbook. The effect size interpretations are summarized in Table 2.2.

When the variables that are used to compare performance are categorical, we must use a different technique. In our example, if we wanted to compare the numbers of students who opted for

TABLE 2.2 Effect Size Interpretation

Effect Size	Interpretation
< .50	Small
.50–1.00	Moderate
> 1.00	Large

advanced classes after completing the current ones, a contingency table would be appropriate. A contingency table shows the results in terms of all possible choices. In our example, a contingency table would show the number of students in both the treatment and comparison groups who opted for advanced courses and those who did not. To compute a contingency table, select the tables icon (**Tables**) on the MYSTAT Main icon bar (see Figure 2.28). This will open a dialog box with a File box, an Add box, several By boxes, and some other options. Select the grouping variable (in our case, **GROUP$**) and move it into the Add box by clicking on **Add→**. Suppose we want to compare the number of students who opted for an advanced course versus those who did not. Highlight the advanced enrollment variable (**ADVENRL$**) and move it to the first By box by clicking on **By→**. The Frequency and Sort categories options are already marked and these should be kept. It is also helpful to include overall percentages and row percentages in our table. This is done by clicking on the boxes beside these two options (**Percent** and **Column percent**). The table is computed by clicking on **OK**. The resulting tables are shown in Figure 2.29.

The analysis produces three tables. The first lists the number of students who met each contingency. For example, 11 students in the treatment group opted for an advanced course, whereas only 2 in the comparison group did. The second table shows these values as percentages of the total number of observations. That is, 37.93% of all the students were in the treatment group and opted for an advanced course, and 6.90% of all the students were in the comparison group and opted for an advanced course. The third table presents the results in terms of column percentages. That is, 73.33% of the students in the treatment group opted for an advanced course,

---

CONSTRUCTING CONTINGENCY TABLES
USING MYSTAT

1. Make sure that the appropriate data set is active.

2. Select the tables icon (**tables**) from the MYSTAT Main icon menu bar to open the tables dialog box.

3. Highlight the grouping variable.

4. Insert the grouping variable into the group box by clicking on **GROUP→**.

5. Click on the name of the second variable to be analyzed (this is usually a grouping variable also).

6. Select **By→** to move the selected variable into the By box.

7. Select the options to be used (Frequency, Percent, Row percent, and Sort categories are recommended).

8. Select **OK** to compute the tables.

9. The results will appear in the MYSTAT Main window.

Figure 2.28. Constructing Contingency Tables Using MYSTAT

whereas only 14.29% of those in the comparison group did. All three tables provide the same information but present it in slightly different ways. All three suggest that more students in the treatment group opted for advanced courses than did students in the comparison group.

The final statistic that we will consider is the correlation coefficient. The correlation coefficient is a numerical measure of a relationship that was graphed using a scatterplot in the last section.

```
TABLE OF ADVENRL$ (ROWS) BY GROUP$ (COLUMNS)

FREQUENCIES

             COMPARSN  TREATMNT      TOTAL
            ---------------------
NO          |    12          4   |    16
            |                    |
YES         |     2         11   |    13
            ---------------------
TOTAL            14         15        29
```

```
TABLE OF ADVENRL$ (ROWS) BY GROUP$ (COLUMNS)

PERCENTS OF TOTAL OF THIS (SUB)TABLE

             COMPARSN  TREATMNT    TOTAL      N
            ---------------------
NO          |  41.38      13.79  |  55.17   16.00
            |                    |
YES         |   6.90      37.93  |  44.83   13.00
            ---------------------
TOTAL          48.28      51.72    100.00
    N            14         15         29
```

```
TABLE OF ADVENRL$ (ROWS) BY GROUP$ (COLUMNS)

COLUMN PERCENTS

             COMPARSN  TREATMNT    TOTAL      N
            ---------------------
NO          |  85.71      26.67  |  55.17   16.00
            |                    |
YES         |  14.29      73.33  |  44.83   13.00
            ---------------------
TOTAL         100.00     100.00    100.00
    N            14         15         29
```

Figure 2.29. Contingency Table for Example

However, a correlation coefficient only measures a linear relationship. Let us begin by computing the correlation coefficient between ACHIEVE and APTITUDE for the treatment group (as is depicted in the scatterplot in Figure 2.20). The first step is to use the Editor

---

COMPUTING CORRELATION COEFFICIENTS

1. Make sure that the appropriate data set is active and the group to be included in the analysis is selected.

2. Select the correlation icon (**Corr**) from the MYSTAT Main icon menu bar to open the Pearson Correlation dialog box.

3. Click on the name of the first variable to be correlated.

4. Select **Add→** to move the selected variable into the Add box.

5. Repeat Steps 3 and 4 with the second variable to be correlated.

6. Select **OK** to compute the correlation coefficient.

7. The results will appear in the MYSTAT Main window.

Figure 2.30. Computing Correlation Coefficients With MYSTAT

in the MYSTAT Worksheet to select the cases in the treatment group (as shown in Figure 2.6). Using the cases that have been identified, select the correlation icon (**Corr**) on the MYSTAT Main icon menu (see Figure 2.30). This will open the Pearson Correlation dialog box. Highlight the two variables of interest (**ACHIEVE** and **APTITUDE**) and click on **Add→**, one at a time, to insert them into the Add box. Click on **OK** and the correlation coefficient will be computed and the results will appear in the MYSTAT Main window (shown in Figure 2.31).

The value that is listed to the right of APTITUDE and under ACHIEVE is 0.943 or .94 rounded off. This represents the linear relationship between the two variables numerically, that is, how closely the cloud of points in a scatterplot can be represented by a

PEARSON CORRELATION MATRIX

	ACHIEVE	APTITUDE
ACHIEVE	1.000	
APTITUDE	0.943	1.000

NUMBER OF OBSERVATIONS: 15

Figure 2.31. MYSTAT Output for Correlation Between ACHIEVE and APTITUDE

straight line. A correlation of .94 is a strong positive relationship as noted in the previous section. A correlation coefficient provides two types of information—the kind of relationship (positive or negative) and the magnitude of the relationship (how strong it is). Correlation coefficients can range from −1.00 (a perfect negative relationship) through 0.00 (no linear relationship) to +1.00 (a perfect positive relationship). Table 2.3 summarizes the types of relationships.

It is possible for data to be related and have a small correlation coefficient. This will happen when the relationship is not linear. For example, if the cloud of points on the scatterplot for two variables fall in a crescent moon shape, the variables have a weak linear relationship, but a strong nonlinear relationship. The model for this type of relationship is beyond the scope of this book.

The Validity of Action Research

Action research is, at the same time, the most valid and the least valid research about classroom practice. Action research is the most valid because it is done in the arena where its results will be used, and it is the least valid when its results are generalized beyond the classroom or classrooms where it was done. Thus one's

TABLE 2.3 Interpreting Correlation Coefficients[a]

Correlation Coefficient	Interpretation
−1.00 to −.70	Strong negative relationship
−.69 to −.40	Moderate negative relationship
−.39 to .39	Weak relationship
.40 to .69	Moderate positive relationship
.70 to 1.00	Strong positive relationship

a. These descriptions apply only to linear relationships and should be used with caution as the interpretation may change under special circumstances.

own action research results probably provide the best information possible about the validity of a process within one's own classroom but may not provide an answer to a problem that can be generalized to a broader arena. For the same reasons, research results that are reported in journals and reported in textbooks may not be valid for every classroom. That is one of the reasons it so important for teachers and administrators to know about action research. Who would spend $20,000 for an automobile without taking a test drive? That is exactly what we often do with our curricula. Action research is the equivalent to test driving an automobile before we purchase it when we are considering a new curriculum, textbook, or any other school innovation. The validity of action research is also dependent on following appropriate procedures such as those presented in this book.

Ethical Considerations

The first rule of ethics in action research in the classroom is "Do no harm." This familiar admonition of physicians is a good rule to follow whether in regard to action research or any other area. This does not mean that we should avoid using comparison groups. The issue of comparison groups is troubling to many action researchers. As noted earlier in this chapter, we can often use archival data, normative data, or data from other teachers or schools as our comparison groups. Even if we were to subdivide our own students to compare achievement, this would not necessarily be an ethical problem as we truly do not know which of our procedures works best. We may suspect that one is better, but if we do not test it out, we may be doing the students a disservice by adopting a new procedure without comparing results with those using the previous procedure.

Some larger school systems may require formal permission to conduct research even in individual classrooms. If such requirements are in effect, by all means, follow them. If procedures are not in place, action research should be discussed with the principal before it is begun if it involves modification of classroom practice. Many action research projects simply involve using data from regular teaching assignments and comparing them to past performance or other standards. Action research is more likely to lead to the fine-tuning rather than the wholesale abandonment of past practice. If a number of teachers in a school or in a district are involved in action research or contemplate involvement, it might be a good idea to set up a school or a district review committee of teachers and administrators. This group could serve to offer suggestions for improving the research and also provide a forum for sharing results as well as reviewing plans. If this is not done formally, informal exchanges among teachers and administrators could serve the same purpose.

Concluding Comments

This chapter provides the substance of action research. It has included an action research strategy and techniques for implementing the strategy in an ethical manner. This chapter includes detailed directions on how to analyze the data that one might obtain from an action research study in a classroom, school, or school system. This strategy and some techniques are illustrated in the next chapter by presenting two detailed examples.

Applying Action Research
at the Classroom, School,
and District Levels

Action research is designed to be applied to educational problems at any level. It can be applied by individual classroom teachers in their own classrooms, by groups of teachers with the support of a principal at the school or building level, or by groups of teachers with the support of a superintendent at the district level. The basic strategies remain the same. The basic difference is that beyond the classroom level, it requires the cooperation of teachers and school administrators. The problems themselves dictate whether a classroom, school, or district approach is more appropriate.

This chapter includes two detailed examples. One was implemented by an individual teacher in his own classroom, and the other was implemented at the district level by a system supervisor with the assistance of cooperating teachers. The second example is similar to what might happen at a school level. In both cases, the three phases of the strategy (conceptualization, implementation, and interpretation) are applied. The difference is that in the first case, they are applied by an individual classroom teacher; in the second case (or third if at the school level), they are applied by more than one cooperating educator.

Example 1: Is Sleep Related to School Achievement?

A high school history teacher, Mr. Ed, observed that students of seemingly equal ability performed very differently on classroom tests. He reasoned that because all students spent the same amount of time in class and had, more or less, the same learning experiences, the differences must be related to out-of-class activities. After observing students closely over a period of time, he noticed that some students seemed rested and alert in class, whereas others seemed sleepy and listless. Mr. Ed wondered if class performance could be related to how much sleep students were getting, and he decided to implement an action research study.

Conceptualization

The conceptualization phase involves identifying the potential inputs and outcomes related to the research. Because the study centered on classroom achievement in general, the inputs were influences that might impact on students both in class and out of class. Mr. Ed reasoned that because the in-class influences were essentially the same for all the students, he would concentrate on the out-of-class events. He identified the following possible out-of-class influences: parental concern, language spoken at home, diet, extracurricular activities, and amount of sleep. The primary language spoken at home was considered potentially important because many of the students' families were first-generation immigrants and the students may not be exposed to English at home. He wanted to include the amount of sleep because of his classroom observations. Mr. Ed decided that he would not include parental influence, diet, and extracurricular activities of the students and that he would concentrate on amount of sleep and the primary language spoken at home as the inputs for the study. He understood that this presented a limitation, but his experience was that the socioeconomic backgrounds of the students' parents were similar and that the literature suggested that students of similar socio-economic levels tended to have similar parental influence and involvement. This was also true of their diets in terms of nutrition.

The general outcome of interest was student achievement. Thus the problem could be conceptualized as, "Are parental influence, language spoken at home, diet, extracurricular activities, and amount of sleep related to achievement?" For analysis purposes, two action research questions were derived from the conceptualization of the problem. These questions were stated as follows:

1. Are students' grades related to the amount of sleep they get?
2. Are students' grades related to whether English is the primary language spoken at home?

Implementation

The first task in completing the implementation phase of the conceptualization was to determine how the variables of the study (inputs and outcomes) would be measured. For a 6-week grading period, Mr. Ed asked the students to keep a log of the amount of sleep (in hours and minutes) that they got each school night. He collected the logs weekly, checking to make sure the information was recorded properly. On the final log, he also asked each student to identify the primary language that was spoken in his or her home (the language spoken more than one half the time). At that time, he averaged the sleep amounts for each student to arrive at a per night average. Mr. Ed decided to use two measures of achievement. The first was the 6-weeks' numerical grade average (a percentage correct scale), and the second was the 6-weeks' letter grade (A, B, C, D, or F). These are related as the number grade scale is used to determine the letter grades, but they provide a slightly different way of viewing the results.

At the end of the 6-week period, Mr. Ed recorded his data in a table similar to Table 3.1.

It is a good practice to begin by describing the data. Recall that we can describe data both graphically and numerically. Figure 3.1 shows the output from the MYSTAT Stats procedure run on the

TABLE 3.1 Data From Sleep Example

Student	Numerical Grade	Letter Grade	Hours of Sleep per Night	English Spoken at Home
1	80	B	8.1	No
2	72	C	7.1	Yes
3	77	C	7.7	No
4	87	B	8.9	No
5	80	B	8.0	Yes
6	96	A	10.0	No
7	92	A	9.5	Yes
8	75	C	7.5	Yes
9	88	B	9.0	No
10	76	C	7.6	No
11	82	B	8.5	Yes
12	58	F	6.1	Yes
13	76	C	7.3	Yes
14	83	B	8.6	No
15	93	A	9.8	Yes
16	78	C	7.9	Yes
17	88	B	11.4	No
18	79	C	8.5	No
19	59	F	7.4	No
20	82	B	8.1	Yes
21	73	C	7.1	Yes
22	74	C	7.5	No
23	82	B	7.9	Yes
24	66	D	6.5	No
25	83	B	8.1	No
26	74	C	7.5	Yes
27	75	C	7.4	No
28	84	B	8.2	Yes
29	65	D	7.3	Yes
30	92	A	8.8	No

```
TOTAL OBSERVATIONS:        30

                        NGRADE          SLEEP

   N OF CASES           30              30
   MINIMUM              58.000           6.100
   MAXIMUM              96.000          11.400
   RANGE                38.000           5.300
   MEAN                 78.967           8.110
   STANDARD DEV          9.342           1.087
   MEDIAN               79.500           7.950
```

Figure 3.1. Descriptive Statistics for Numerical Grade and Amount of Sleep

sleep and numerical grade variables. Figure 3.2 shows the results from the MYSTAT Tables procedure run on the letter grade and English spoken at home variables.

The numerical grades range from 58 to 96, with a mean and standard deviation of 78.97 and 9.34, respectively. The average amount of sleep students got per night ranged from 6.1 hours to 11.4 hours, with a mean of 8.11 hours and a standard deviation of 1.09 hours. Letter grades ranged from A to F, with most students getting Bs and Cs. The same number of students had English as the primary language in their households as those who had other languages.

Graphical procedures can be used to show similar information. Figure 3.3 shows the stem-and-leaf graphs for the same data using the MYSTAT Stem procedure. Note that the stem-and-leaf graphs also provide information on the hinges and outliers in the data sets. The outliers should be checked to make sure they are legitimate data points.

Now, let us answer the action research questions. To address the first question, "Are students' grades related to the amount of sleep they get?" requires two analyses, one for the grades measured on the numerical scale and another for the grades measured on the letter scale. The numerical grades can be analyzed graphically by constructing a scatterplot or numerically by computing a correlation coefficient. Because both numerical grades and amount of sleep are

```
TABLE OF ENGLISH$ (ROWS) BY LTRGRAD$ (COLUMNS)

FREQUENCIES

            A       B       C       D       F    TOTAL
      -------------------------------------------------
NO  |       2       6       5       1       1  |    15
    |                                          |
YES |       2       5       6       1       1  |    15
      -------------------------------------------------
TOTAL       4      11      11       2       2       30
```

```
TABLE OF ENGLISH$ (ROWS) BY LTRGRAD$ (COLUMNS)

PERCENTS OF TOTAL OF THIS (SUB)TABLE

            A       B       C       D       F    TOTAL
      -------------------------------------------------
NO  |    6.67   20.00   16.67    3.33    3.33 |  50.00
    |                                          |
YES |    6.67   16.67   20.00    3.33    3.33 |  50.00
      -------------------------------------------------
TOTAL   13.33   36.67   36.67    6.67    6.67   100.00
```

```
TABLE OF  ENGLISH$ (ROWS) BY LTRGRAD$ (COLUMNS)

COLUMN PERCENTS

            A       B       C       D       F    TOTAL
      -------------------------------------------------
NO  |   50.00   54.55   45.45   50.00   50.00|  50.00
    |                                         |
YES |   50.00   45.45   54.55   50.00   50.00|  50.00
      -------------------------------------------------
TOTAL  100.00  100.00  100.00  100.00  100.00  100.00
```

Figure 3.2. Frequencies and Percentages of Letter Grades by Primary Language Spoken in the Home Generated by MYSTAT

NUMERICAL GRADES

```
5  8
   •••OUTSIDE VALUES•••
5  9
6
6  56
7H 2334
7M 5566789
8H 00222334
8  788
9  223
9  6
```

AMOUNT OF SLEEP

```
6  1
6  5
7H 113344
7M 5556699
8  01112
8H 55689
9  0
9  589
   •••OUTSIDE VALUES•••
11  4
```

Figure 3.3. Stem-and-Leaf Graphs of Numerical Grades and Amount of Sleep

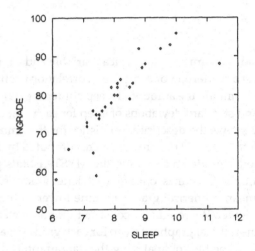

Figure 3.4. Scatterplot of the Relationship Between Numerical Grades and Amount of Sleep

numerical scores, the MYSTAT Plot and Corr procedures do the analyses as directed in Chapter 2. The resulting scatterplot is shown in Figure 3.4.

The correlation coefficient was computed to be .84. Note that both the scatterplot and the correlation coefficient of .84 suggest a strong positive relationship between students' grades and the amount of sleep they get.

TABLE 3.2 Descriptive Statistics for Amount of Sleep by Letter Grade

Grade	N	Mean	Standard Deviation
A	4	9.52	.53
B	11	8.62	.99
C	11	7.55	.39
D	2	6.90	.57
F	2	6.75	.92

The letter grades comprise a categorical variable and cannot be used to construct a scatterplot or compute a correlation coefficient. Instead, we can compare the amount of sleep students get by computing means and standard deviations of sleep for each grade separately. Table 3.2 shows the descriptive statistics for the amount of sleep for each letter grade. These results were computed by selecting a specific letter grade and running the MYSTAT Stats procedure. It had to be run five times, once for each letter grade selected. Note that the mean numerical grades become lower as the letter grades become lower. We could also construct graphs such as histograms or stem-and-leaf graphs of sleep for each grade separately. A more expedient method of analyzing the data graphically is to construct a box plot of sleep for each letter grade. This can be done with one procedure using MYSTAT Box. Figure 3.5 depicts the results from such an analysis. Again, it can be seen that the numerical grades generally become lower as the amount of sleep decreases. The box plots also show how these groups seem to overlap slightly and that there are outliers in the B and C groups.

The second action research question was, "Are students' grades related to whether English is the primary language spoken at home?" Again, this was analyzed twice, once for numerical grades and again for letter grades. We will use the MYSTAT box and t-test procedures to examine the numerical grades for students from English and non-English households. The box plots are shown in Figure 3.6.

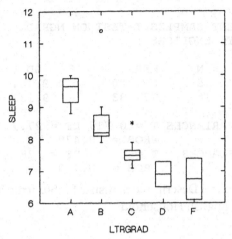

Figure 3.5. Box Plots of Amount of Sleep by Letter Grade

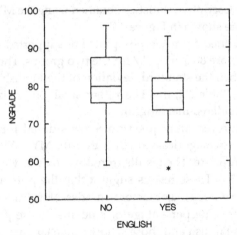

Figure 3.6. Box Plots of Numerical Grades for Students From English and Non-English Households

It can be seen from the box plots that the two sets of data overlap considerably. In fact, students from households that do not speak English have slightly higher numerical scores. It should also be noted that there is an outlier in the English household group. It

```
INDEPENDENT SAMPLES T-TEST ON NGRADE
GROUPED BY   ENGLISH$

GROUP        N       MEAN              SD
NO          15      80.200           9.704
YES         15      77.733           9.130

SEPARATE VARIANCES T = 0.717 DF = 27.9
                   PROB =  0.479
POOLED VARIANCES   T = 0.717 DF =  28
                   PROB =  0.479
```

Figure 3.7. Numerical Descriptive Statistics for Students from English and Non-English Households

would be difficult to conclude that grades are related to what the primary language is at home because the graphs have such overlap.

The numerical descriptive statistics obtained using the MYSTAT t-test procedure are shown in Figure 3.7.

The results obtained from the box plots are supported by the means. The means are 80.2 and 77.7 for the two groups. The effect size is only .27 when the standard deviation of the English group is used. Based on Table 2.2, this is a rather small effect size and should not be considered meaningful.

When the action research question is considered for letter grades, we have two categorical variables, thus the MYSTAT Tables procedure is appropriate. The results from this analysis were presented in Figure 3.2. These results suggest that the primary language in the home is not a major factor in grades. Note from Figure 3.2 that about the same percentage of students whose primary home language is English and those whose home language is not earned each grade.

Interpretation

The interpretation of the results is, essentially, answering the action research questions. The first action research question is answered, yes, grades are related to the amount of sleep students are getting. This is supported by both the graphical analyses and the numerical analyses. The numerical grades are strongly and positively related to the average amount of sleep per night, and this can be seen graphically in Figure 3.4. In other words, as students get more sleep, their achievement increases. This conclusion is also supported by the results of the mean amount of sleep reported for each letter grade in Table 3.2 and the box plots of the amount of sleep for each letter grade reported in Figure 3.5.

The answer to the second action research question is, no, the primary language spoken in the home does not seem to be related to student achievement as measured by grades. Again, both the numerical and graphical analyses support this result. The analyses of the numerical grades reported in Figures 3.6 and 3.7 show very little relationship. This is further supported by the analyses of the letter grades reported in Figure 3.2.

For the students in this particular classroom, it can be concluded that sleep is related to achievement and the primary language in the home is not related to achievement. If the conceptual phase of this study was correct, Mr. Ed should examine sleep further. Be aware that even though two variables are related to one another, this does not necessarily mean that one caused the other. In other words, because the amount of sleep and achievement are positively related, it does not mean that increasing the amount of sleep will increase grades. However, if there is no relationship, then one variable did not cause the other to change, as with grades and the primary language spoken at home. These results do suggest that a causal relationship is possible and more work needs to be done.

As stated previously, action research is not a quick fix but a process that must be sustained to be effective. In the case of Mr. Ed, he must implement another action research study to see if, indeed, increasing the amount of sleep students get does increase their achievement. This would entail designing an intervention with the students and/or their parents to increase the amount of sleep and then studying the results. He might want to use another class as a comparison group, using the intervention in one class but collecting data from both classes. Action research is a cyclical process in which we are searching for a better way.

Example 2: Self-Contained Versus Rotating Classes

Let us turn our attention to an example that was done at a school district level. The procedures are the same as if it was done at the school level. In this example, Dr. Martinez, the curriculum supervisor at the school district, was exploring ways of improving the achievement of middle school students. The system included seven middle schools with Grades 6, 7, and 8. Each of the schools used a class rotation schedule where children changed classes six times a day. Dr. Martinez studied the middle school literature and found that many researchers recommend self-contained classes for children in this age group. She was interested in determining if self-contained classes would improve achievement in her district.

Conceptualization

The problem was that of comparing the achievement of middle school children on a class rotation schedule with those in self-contained classes. The district used state-adopted textbooks with a state-approved curriculum. No change was anticipated in these arrangements.

Dr. Martinez asked the eighth-grade teachers to attend a meeting to discuss the possibility of changing to self-contained classes. After a thorough discussion of the potential advantages and disadvantages, 16 teachers volunteered to move to self-contained classes the following year. Dr. Martinez recognized that a fair study of self-contained classes would need a comparison group. Therefore, she randomly selected eight of the teachers to move to self-contained classes by putting all 16 names on slips of paper and drawing them out of a hat. She committed to the other eight teachers that they would have the opportunity to switch the following year if they were still interested. In the meantime, she arranged for a 4-week course on self-contained classes for the eight teachers who were chosen to participate. It was agreed that the curriculum would remain the same for students using both the rotation schedule and self-contained classes. The difference would be that the students in self-contained classes would stay with one teacher for all of their subjects except physical education and music and the others would follow the current rotating class schedule.

The purpose of the action research was to determine if students in self-contained classes improved their achievement more than did students in a class rotation arrangement. Because this could be related to several subjects, Dr. Martinez decided to consider three action research questions. They were as follows:

1. Does the achievement of students in reading improve more when they attend self-contained classes or rotate among classes?
2. Does the achievement of students in mathematics improve more when they attend self-contained classes or rotate among classes?
3. Does the achievement of students in language improve more when they attend self-contained classes or rotate among classes?

Implementation

The action research study was designed so that selected students from the teachers who were in self-contained classes participated as well as students of teachers who had volunteered to participate but were not selected. This controlled for a possible "volunteer" effect. As noted, the teachers of the self-contained classes received extensive training in how it should be done. About 50 students from each group were selected to participate. They were selected in the same way as the teachers; that is, names were put on slips of paper and drawn at random for the two groups.

It was decided to use the standardized tests to measure student achievement. This district gives the Stanford Achievement Tests (SAT) near the end of each school year. Therefore, each student would have SAT scores at the end of the year before the study and at the end of the year of the study. Thus a gain score could be computed for each student. It was also decided to use the SAT Total Reading (READ), Total Mathematics (MATH), and Total Language (LANG) scaled scores as the measures because scaled scores are comparable across years and forms of the test.

TABLE 3.3 Descriptive Statistics for Classroom
Organization Study

		Pretest			Posttest		
Group	Subject	N	Mean	SD	N	Mean	SD
	Reading	49	673.1	34.32	52	674.9	37.67
Rotate	Math	52	659.0	38.73	51	697.2	27.38
	Language	48	630.6	30.53	52	656.5	27.04
	Reading	44	655.4	38.17	47	676.3	60.70
Self-Contained	Math	45	660.1	32.17	44	672.4	31.48
	Language	46	627.5	30.14	46	654.5	29.08

At the end of the study year, data were collected and recorded
for 99 students (52 who rotated classes and 47 who were in self-
contained classes). Both the scores from the end of the previous
year (Pre) and the end of the present year (Post) were recorded.
MYSTAT was used to compute the Gain scores for each student by
subtracting their prescores from the postscores for each student.
This was done using the Editor on the MYSTAT Worksheet by selecting Math from the Editor menu and inserting the following
equation into the Variable boxes: READGAIN=READPOST–
READPRE. READPOST and READPRE were the names given to
the reading posttest and pretest scores, respectively, and READGAIN
was the name assigned to the reading gain score. This process was
repeated for math and language. Before addressing the action research questions, descriptive statistics were computed for the pre-
and posttest scores in both groups. These were computed using the
Select cases feature of the MYSTAT Worksheet editor followed by
the Stats procedure from the MYSTAT Main icon menu. The results
are summarized in Table 3.3. Because some students were absent
when the pretest or posttest was given in a particular subject, the
sample sizes (N) are not the same. MYSTAT automatically deletes
these cases during analysis.

These data can also be examined graphically. Figure 3.8 shows
the box plots for each set of data.

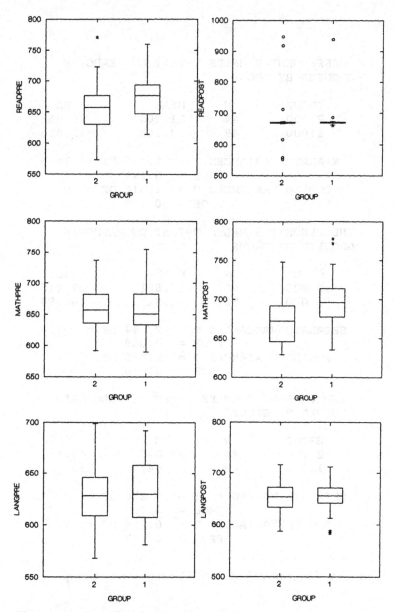

Figure 3.8. Box Plots for Reading, Math, and Language Pretest and Posttest Scores by Group

```
INDEPENDENT SAMPLES T-TEST ON READGAIN
GROUPED BY GROUP

       GROUP        N      MEAN              SD
       2.000       44    21.205          70.451
       1.000       49     2.163          49.855

SEPARATE VARIANCES T =   1.489 DF =   76.5
             PROB =   0.141
  POOLED VARIANCES T =   1.516 DF =   91
             PROB =   0.133

INDEPENDENT SAMPLES T-TEST ON MATHGAIN
GROUPED BY GROUP

       GROUP        N      MEAN              SD
       2.000       42    13.881          39.446
       1.000       51    37.941          46.997

SEPARATE VARIANCES T =  -2.684 DF =   91.0
             PROB =   0.009
  POOLED VARIANCES T =  -2.639 DF =   91
             PROB =   0.010

INDEPENDENT SAMPLES T-TEST ON LANGGAIN
GROUPED BY GROUP

       GROUP        N      MEAN              SD
       2.000       45    27.044          43.154
       1.000       48    25.042          30.931

SEPARATE VARIANCES T =   0.256 DF =   79.4
             PROB =   0.799
  POOLED VARIANCES T =   0.258 DF =   91
             PROB =   0.797
```

Figure 3.9. Descriptive Statistics of Gain Scores by Group

Now we are ready to compare the gain scores of the rotating schedule group with those of the self-contained group. Again, this can be done both numerically and graphically. Figure 3.9 presents

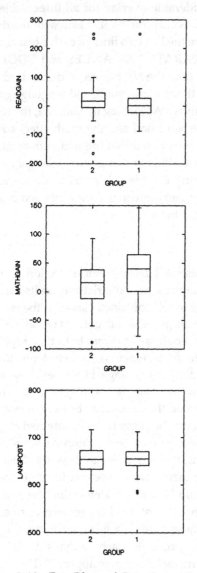

Figure 3.10. Box Plots of Gain Scores by Group

the gain score statistics by group obtained using the MYSTAT t-test procedure and Figure 3.10 shows the box plots by group.

The box plots show considerable overlap for all three subjects. Using the t-test results, we can compute the effect sizes for the three subjects. Remember to ignore the last two lines of each t-test analysis (the ones that start SEPARATE VARIANCES and POOLED VARIANCES) and consider only the Ns, means, and standard deviations. The effect sizes for the reading, math, and language gains are .38, –.51, and .06, respectively. According to Table 2.2, the reading and language effect sizes are small and the math effect size is only moderate. It should also be noted that the math effect size is negative. Because we subtracted the rotation group mean gain from the self-contained group mean gain, this indicates that the students who rotated classes did better than those in the self-contained classes on the mathematics portion of the test.

Interpretation

Based on the results as presented in the previous section, should Dr. Martinez recommend that the school district stay on its current rotational schedule or change to self-contained classes at the eighth-grade level? This is a good example of where general research findings may not apply to a specific situation. From both the graphical and numerical analyses of the achievement scores, students do not do appreciably better in reading or language. However, they seem to do better in mathematics when using the rotating class schedule.

It is important to keep in mind that there may be very important social or behavioral reasons for changing to self-contained classes (these reasons could also be explored with action research). But with respect to achievement, the action research study does not support such a change. If the change were to be considered for other reasons, action research could be used to determine the reasons students do not do as well in self-contained classes as on a rotating schedule. For example, because math is a more technical subject, do the students benefit from specialists teaching that subject? This illustrates how action research is not a one-time approach. The results of one action research study often suggest other studies. Action research is an ongoing search for what works best.

Summary

The two examples illustrate how action research can be applied to the classroom or school district levels. The same techniques work equally well at the school level. Generally, the school level is more similar to district level action research than to classroom level. However, the same strategies are employed at both levels.

Both examples also illustrate another principle of action research. That is, action research is not merely one study, but a step in the process of school improvement. In the classroom example, note how possible changes to improve student sleep time would need to be explored, not only in terms of whether they increased the amount of sleep students got but also whether these changes translated into improved achievement. In the classroom organization study, no matter which approach the curriculum supervisor and teachers choose, other questions are raised about their impact.

Both examples illustrate how little additional information needs to be collected to conduct action research. In the classroom example, students were asked to keep a simple log. In the classroom organization example, no new information was needed as it used test data that were already collected. In both cases, the additional work related to the analyses of the data. The examples also illustrated how one can use prior research (as in the classroom organization example) or personal observation (as in the amount-of-sleep example) to suggest the action research questions. Both are equally valid. In fact, most studies begin with a personal observation by a teacher or administrator that is refined by examining the literature on the topic. This takes best advantage of both approaches. Regardless of which approach is used, action research is the most valid process for determining what works best in a particular situation.

Improving Education
Through Action Research

This book has presented a strategy for action research and the techniques needed to implement the strategy. This chapter summarizes the approach in terms of a model for action research and discusses the potential of action research.

An Action Research Model

A strategy for action research and the methods of implementing this strategy have already been presented. The information is summarized in this chapter in terms of an action research model. Figure 4.1 presents an action research model that incorporates the strategy and its implementation process.

The action research model depicted in Figure 4.1 is essentially the action research strategy combined with the implementation suggestions presented in Chapter 2. There is one very important addition to the model. The model does not have a specific beginning and a specific end. It is circular. That is, when one cycle of action research is completed, another begins. In fact, action research is

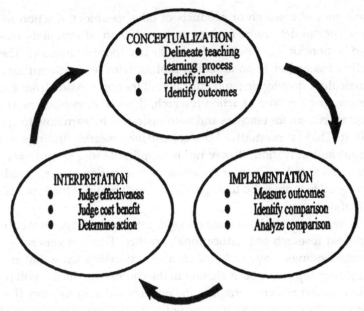

Figure 4.1. Action Research Model

most effective when it is a continuous approach to improving the achievement and other outcomes of education. The model suggests that teachers and administrators who employ action research will always be involved in some phase of the process. It really does not end, but new research questions are considered as old ones are resolved.

The Potential of Action Research

Action research has the potential to improve education as does no educational innovation of the past century. Action research is not a program or specific intervention, but a process for improvement. It arms every teacher and administrator with the skills and attitude not to accept the status quo but to ask, "Is there a better way?" A teacher or administrator knowledgeable of action research feels empowered because he or she is no longer merely the consumer of research or products of other people; the action researcher can determine for him- or herself if an educational practice is more or less effective for his or her specific situation. The action researcher is on an equal footing with textbook authors, curriculum developers, and educational theorists. Aside from the empowering nature of action research, there is an even more important reason for teachers and administrators to learn how to apply it. That is, no matter how conclusive research findings are about an innovation, it may not be applicable in a specific situation. As noted in Chapter 2, the results from action research studies are often more valid than general research findings for a specific situation.

Action research should be a necessary step between general educational research and educational practice. Because general research findings may not fit all situations, it makes sense that any educational process be evaluated in the context in which it will be used. Action research provides the perfect model for this practice. Using action research in this way not only evaluates the validity of the process under study but also promotes a greater understanding of the practice by the teachers and administrators studying it. If the practice is not evaluated as effective by the action research process, chances are that the action researchers can suggest modifications that will make it effective. The process of action research also establishes a peer relationship with educational theorists and researchers rather than a producer/consumer relationship as was true in the past.

The primary benefit of action research is the personal satisfaction that is derived from providing more control over one's professional life and improving the educational environment for students. Action research, by its nature, is a teacher- and administrator-empowering process. The implementation of an action research agenda empowers the action researchers to use their inquiry skills, identify best practice, and help determine what is best for their classrooms and schools. In a sense, they become masters of their own classrooms and schools. In doing so, the school and school system benefits from the full measure of the creativity of all teachers and administrators. In the end, the children benefit from a better education and society benefits from a better educated populace.

Annotated Bibliography
and References

Allen, J., & Shockley, B. (1994, April). *Becoming a community of researchers, evaluation of a school research consortium.* Paper presented at the annual meeting of the American Educational Research Association, New Orleans, LA.

This paper makes a case for the use of school-based research. Specifically, the perspective of this paper is that although knowledge produced by teachers is often dismissed as anecdotal, local, and not rigorous, and university-based research is perceived as authoritative because it is systematic, scientific, and generalizable, school-based research provides an essential, viable, and valuable research perspective.

Berk, K. E. (1994). *Data analysis with Student SYSTAT.* Cambridge, MA: Course Technology, Inc.

A copy of the Student SYSTAT software accompanies this book. In fact, the book was designed to teach the use of SYSTAT and data analysis together. It comes in DOS, Windows, and Macintosh versions. The cost is about $50, including the Student SYSTAT software and the set of examples used in the book. The book is an excellent elementary to intermediate statistics text as well as a manual for Student SYSTAT. Student SYSTAT includes many of the same features as the full SYSTAT but with *some limitations. The most obvious of these is multivariate statistics. For the purposes of the present book on action research, this is of no concern. The book can be purchased from Course Technology, Inc., One Main Street, Cambridge, MA 02142, tel. 800-543-7972.*

Burton, F. R. (1986). Research currents: A teacher's conception of the action research process. *Language Arts, 63,* 718-723.

Burton, an elementary school teacher in Columbus, Ohio, provides his personal views of action research. He organizes his discussion around the foundations of action research, the action research process itself, and reflections. Burton refers to "reflection" as the "soul of action." He uses examples from his own classrooms to illustrate his points.

Cameron-Jones, M. (1983, December). *A researching profession? The growth of classroom action research.* Paper presented at the Seminar on Pedagogy, Glasgow, Scotland. (ERIC Document Reproduction Service No. ED 266 138)

This paper is an excellent introduction to action research. It begins with a short history of action research and provides a general model. Some examples of action research are explored, followed by a discussion of how action research might contribute to education in Scotland. However, its conclusions—specifically, that action research contributes to staff development and to the theory and practice of education—are equally applicable to the United States.

Cook, S. W. (1984, April). *Action research: Its origins and early application.* Paper presented at the annual meeting of the American Educational Research Association, Toronto, Canada. (ERIC Document Reproduction Service No. ED 253 544)

Cook, a social psychologist, provides a look at the beginnings of what has come to be called action research and provides a history of its early development and decline. The paper also points out a number of major issues that examined the successful use of action research in the 1940s and 1950s.

Educational action research. (1993). Triangle Journals Ltd., Wallingford, Oxfordshire, United Kingdom.

This is a peer-refereed journal devoted entirely to educational action research. It is published three times per year and includes *accounts of action research and development studies and contributions to the debate on the theory and practice of action research and associated methodologies. It welcomes contributions from practitioner researchers in schools, higher education, educational administration, social work, and so on. Subscriptions can be obtained by writing Triangle Journals Ltd., P.O. Box 65, Wallingford, Oxfordshire OX10 0YG, United Kingdom. Individual subscriptions are US$55.*

Eisenhart, M., & Borko, H. (1993). *Designing classroom research: Themes, issues, and struggles.* Needham Heights, MA: Allyn & Bacon.

This book reviews the contributions of psychology and anthropology to action research and provides numerous examples. Its greatest contribution may be the chapter, "Standards of Validity for Classroom Research" that identifies five standards by which to judge the validity of classroom research. It also has an excellent section on the validity of classroom research.

Hale, R. L. (1992). *MYSTAT statistical applications.* Cambridge, MA: Course Technology, Inc.

This book comes with a copy of the MYSTAT software. As with Student SYSTAT, the book was designed to teach the use of MYSTAT and data analysis together. It comes in DOS, Windows, and Macintosh versions (the senior author of the Windows edition is J. W. Steagall). The cost is about $20, including the MYSTAT software and the set of examples used in the book. The book is an excellent elementary statistics text as well as a manual for MYSTAT. MYSTAT is a proper subset of SYSTAT and Student SYSTAT with many of the same features. However, it does have limitations on the features it includes as well as the number of variables it will handle. For the purposes of the present book on action research, this is not a limitation. The book can be purchased from Course Technology, Inc., One Main Street, Cambridge, MA 02142, tel. 800-543-7972.

Miller, D. M., & Pine, G. J. (1990). Advancing professional inquiry for educational improvement through action research. *Journal of Staff Development, 11*(3), 56-61.

The major theme of this article is that action research is a staff development process that advances the professional development of teachers. It provides examples of how this happens and provides a continuum of approaches to professional development

that illustrate the differences between traditional staff develop-
ment and project-based staff development.

O'Connor, B. N. (1990). About action research versus formal research. *Business Education Forum, 44*(4), 8-9.

This short article begins with the question, "Does 'action' re-
search have greater promise/potential in solving school policy
problems than formal research?" It leads the reader through a
seven-step action research process and then compares action re-
search with formal research. Finally, the article concludes that
action research does not necessary have greater potential than
formal research, but the choice between action and formal
should be based on the situation. Indeed, action research can be
just as effective.

SPSS Inc. (1992), *SYSTAT* (Version 5) [Computer program]. Chicago,
IL: SPSS Inc. (Formerly available from SYSTAT, Inc., Evanston,
IL)

SYSTAT is a complete statistical package that will meet the data
analysis needs for all but the most demanding analyses. It is
available in DOS, Windows, and Macintosh versions and can
be used easily by a person who is familiar with MYSTAT or
Student SYSTAT. In addition, SYSTAT has the capability to
import data directly from MYSTAT, Student SYSTAT, or a
number of other sources. SYSTAT is considerably more expen-
sive than MYSTAT or Student SYSTAT but includes excellent
documentation (separate books for getting started, statistics,
data entry and manipulation, and graphics) and technical sup-
port. SYSTAT can be purchased from SPSS Inc., 444 N. Michi-
gan Avenue, Chicago, IL 60611, tel. 800-543-2185.

Steagall, J. W., & Hale, R. L. (1994). *MYSTAT for Windows.* Cambridge,
MA: Course Technology, Inc.

(See Hale, 1992, for more information.)

Wick, J. W. (1987). *School-based evaluation.* Boston: Kluwer-Nijhoff.

This book provides a practical approach to school-level-oriented
research. In addition to a step-by-step process, the book provides
many examples of school research ranging from kindergarten
through high school.